FROM VIKINGS TO MODERN LIVING

Geography of Norway

Children's Geography & Culture Books

BABY PROFESSOR
EDUCATION KIDS

Speedy Publishing LLC

40 E. Main St. #1156

Newark, DE 19711

www.speedypublishing.com

Copyright 2017

Norway is a country that is located on the Continent of Europe. At 323,802 km, it is somewhat larger than the state of New Mexico. In this book, we will be learning about this country's history, its people, and its economy.

THE HISTORY OF NORWAY

Norway is probably most known for its Viking Age which took place from the 9th century to the 11th century. This era started during the late 800s once King Harald Fairhair, the first Viking, united the Vikings into one nation. As a seafaring people, the Vikings were able to expand their territory and raid the northern part of Europe.

Replica of the first church in Greenland

They settle most of Greenland and parts of Ireland and Britain. Olav I became Norway's first Christian king during the 11th century and during his reign, converted most of Norway to Christianity.

Norway united with Sweden and Denmark in 1397 under the Kalmar Union. In 1521, Sweden broke away from this union, but Norway became part of the Danish Kingdom in 1586. Norway was taken from Denmark after the Napoleonic wars and under the Treaty of Kiel, became combined with Sweden in 1814. Norway again gained its independence in 1905.

Battle of the Napoleonic Wars

World War 1

During World War I, Norway remained neutral, but the Germans occupied the country during World War II. Norway became one of the founding members of the United Nations after this war. It is not part of the European Union.

WHO WERE THE VIKINGS?

The Vikings were the people that lived during the Middle Ages in Northern Europe. Originally, they had settled in the Scandinavian lands known today as Norway, Sweden, and Denmark. They played a key role during the Middle Ages, particularly during the Viking Age which occurred from 800 CE to 1066 CE.

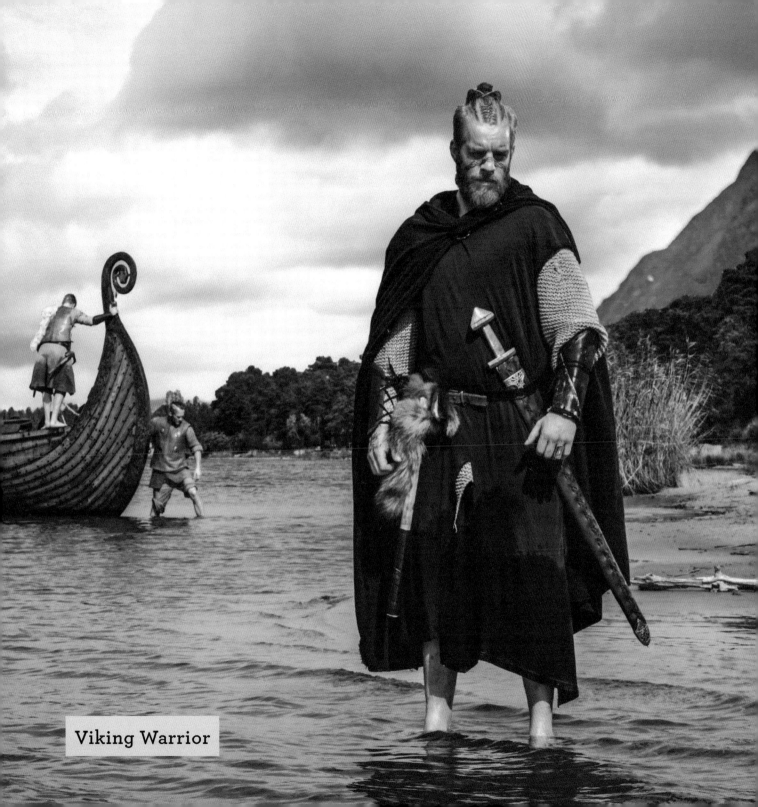

Viking Warrior

VIKING RAIDS

In Old Norse, the term Viking actually does mean "to raid". They would board their ships, and go across the waters, raiding villages along Europe's northern coast, including the islands of Scotland and Great Britain. It was in 787 CE that they first appeared in England and raided the villages. They were known to raid the defenseless monasteries and they had a bad reputation as barbarians. However, the Vikings knew that the monasteries were wealthy and easy targets.

THE VIKING AGE AND EXPANSION INTO EUROPE

The Vikings eventually started settling in the lands outside of Scandinavia. They settled areas of Iceland, Germany, Scotland, and Great Britain during the 9th century. During the 10th century they proceeded into northeastern Europe, as well as Russia. They then settled along France's northern coast, which is where Normandy was established. The term Normandy means "northmen".

Scandinavia

Statue of Leif Eriksson

The Vikings were at the top of their expansion by the beginning of the 11th century. Leif Eriksson, who was the Viking son of Erik the Red, would actually make it to the land we know as North America hundreds and hundreds of years prior to Columbus' arrival. His short settlement was located in what we now know as Canada.

THE END OF THE VIKING AGE

Led by Norway's King Harald Hardrada, the Vikings lost to the English and King Harold Godwinson in 1066. This battle loss is often referred to as the end of the Viking Age. The Vikings had now stopped seeking to expand their territory and their raids became less frequent.

Viking Ships

Old wooden church, Scandinavia

The coming of Christianity was one of the main reasons for the demise of the Viking Age. Scandinavia had converted to Christianity and was now a part of Christian Europe, and the Vikings were becoming more part of mainland Europe. In addition, the boundaries and identity of Norway, Denmark, and Sweden were starting to form.

VIKING SHIPS

The Vikings were probably most famous for their long ships, which they made to explore and to raid. The Viking longships were narrow and long, designed to be fast. Typically, they were propelled with oars, but would later include sails for help during windy conditions. They consisted of a shallow draft which meant they were able to float in shallow water, which made them great for landing on the beaches along the coast of the different countries.

Viking Longship

They also built cargo ships known as knarrs which were used for trading. It was deeper and wider so that it was able to carry the weight of additional cargo.

In Roskilde, Denmark, there is a Viking Ship Museum which exhibits five Viking ships that have been recovered and you can see how the Viking ships were built. They used the clinker building method for building their ships, using longs wood planks overlapping along the edges.

Roskilde in Denmark

Kalmar Castle

THE KALMAR UNION

In 1319, Magnus Erikson, at the young age of 3, inherited the throne after the death of the King of Norway, Haakon V, and became King Magnus VII of Norway. During this same time, an attempt to make him King of Sweden was a success, and both the kings of Denmark and Sweden were elected by their individual nobles. With his victory in Sweden, both Norway and Sweden became united under his rule.

The Black Death drastically altered the country of Norway in 1349, killing somewhere between 50 to 60 percent of the country's population and left it in a period of economic and social decline, and left the country very poor. Even though the rate of death was similar with the rest of Europe, Norway's economic recovery took a lot longer due to its scattered, small population. Its population was only approximately 500,000 before the plague.

Old Viking Farm

Many farms remained idle after the plague while its population started to slowly increase. The few tenants of the surviving farms, however, discovered that their bargaining positions with the landlords became greatly strengthened.

King Magnus VII would rule Norway until 1350 when Haakon, his son, was crowned Haakon VI. Haakon VI married Margaret in 1363. She was the daughter of the King of Denmark, King Valdemar IV. When Haakon VI died in 1379 Olav IV, his son, was ten years old. On May 3, 1376, Olaf had been elected to the throne.

Medieval stone church built on the order of King Magnus

Haakon's Hall

Consequently, upon the accession of the throne of Norway to Olaf, Norway and Denmark entered into a personal union. Queen Margaret, who was Haakon's widow and Olaf's mother, would take care of the foreign affairs of Norway and Denmark until Olaf IV became of age.

Margaret began working to create a union of Sweden with Norway and Denmark by getting Olaf elected to the Swedish throne. She was close to achieving this when he died suddenly. Denmark proceeded to make Margaret the temporary ruler upon Olaf's death. Norway followed and crowned Margaret as the Queen on February 2, 1388.

Margaret of Denmark

Eric of Pomerania

She realized that if she could find a king to take over for her, that her power would be more secure. She settled on the grandson of her sister, Eric of Pomerania. Thus, Eric of Pomerania would be crowned as king of all three of the Scandinavian countries at a meeting held at Kalmar.

THE DISSOLUTION OF THE UNION

A shipping magnate and statesman known as Christian Michelson, play a main role in the Norway's peaceful separation from Sweden on June 7, 1905. The people's desire for a monarchy over a republic was confirmed by a national referendum. There was not any Norwegian that could claim the throne legitimately since none could prove any relationship to medieval royalty.

Kalmar Castle

Statue of King Haakon VII

The throne of Norway was offered by the government to a prince from the Dano-German royal house of Schleswig-Holstein-Sonderburg-Glücksburg. Denmark's Prince Carl was elected unanimously as king, becoming the first king of a Norway for 508 years. He became Haakon VII. The country welcomed him, his wife Maude, and their young son in 1905.

POST-WORLD WAR II

The Labour Party maintained an absolute majority from 1945 to 1962. Led by prime minister Gerhardsen, the government started a program that was inspired by Keynesian economics, which emphasized industrialization that was financed by the state and cooperation between employers' organizations and trade unions. In 1949, the rationing of dairy products was lifted, but price control and rationing of cars and housing went on until about 1960.

Einar Gerhardsen

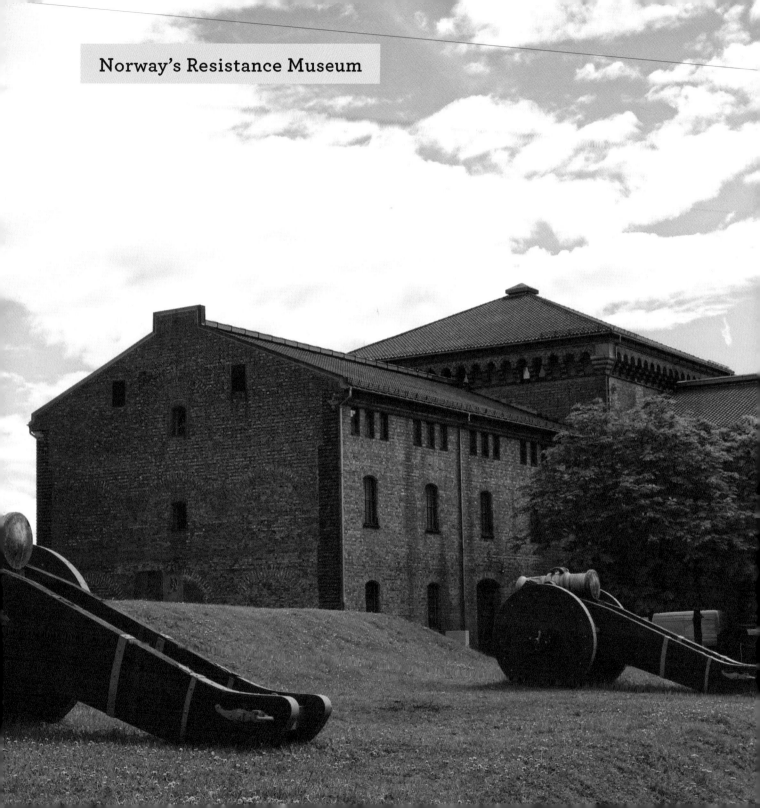

The wartime alliance between the United States and the United Kingdom continued during the post-war years. The Labour Party began distancing from the Communists and strengthened their foreign policy as well as the defense ties with the United States. In 1947, Norway obtained Marshall Plan aid from the United States, one year later joined the OEEC, and then in 1949 became one of the founding members of NATO (North Atlantic Treaty Organization).

The Phillips Petroleum Company found petroleum resources located at Ekofisk field in 1969. The Norwegian government, in 1973, founded Statoil, the State oil company. However, production of oil didn't provide any net income until early in the 1980s due to the huge capital investment required to establish the petroleum industry. By 1975, both the absolute number of workers and the proportion of workers peaked.

Ekofisk Complex

Oslo Parliament in Norway

The first prime minister of Norway, Gro Harlem Brundtland of the Labour party, proceeded with several of the reforms of her predecessor, still backing traditional Labour concerns that included high taxes, social security, feminism, and the industrialization of nature. Norway had paid its foreign debt by the late 1990s, and began accumulating a sovereign wealth fund.

Norway suffered two terrorist attacks in 2011, both occurring on the same day. These attacks were led by Anders Behring Breivik, striking in the government quarter of Oslo as well as at Utøya island, at a the Labour party's youth movement summer camp, which resulted in 319 wounded and 77 deaths.

Utoya Island

Lofoten, Norway

The history of Norway is quite interesting, from the Vikings to the young rulers. Can you imagine ruling a country at ten years old?

For additional information about Norway you can go to your local library, research the internet, and ask questions of your teachers, family and friends.

Visit

BABY PROFESSOR
EDUCATION KIDS

www.BabyProfessorBooks.com

to download Free Baby Professor eBooks
and view our catalog of new and exciting
Children's Books

Printed in Great Britain
by Amazon